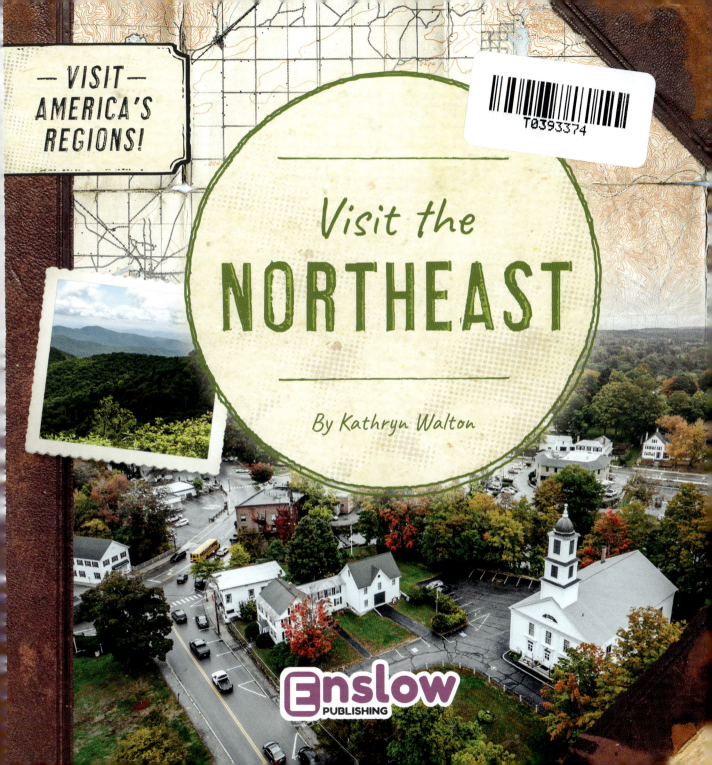

Please visit our website, www.enslow.com. For a free color catalog of all our high-quality books, call toll free 1-800-398-2504 or fax 1-877-980-4454.

Library of Congress Cataloging-in-Publication Data
Names: Walton, Kathryn, 1993- author.
Title: Visit the Northeast / Kathryn Walton.
Description: Buffalo, NY : Enslow Publishing, [2024] | Series: Visit America's regions! | Includes bibliographical references and index.
Identifiers: LCCN 2023033342 (print) | LCCN 2023033343 (ebook) | ISBN 9781978537545 (library binding) | ISBN 9781978537538 (paperback) | ISBN 9781978537552 (ebook)
Subjects: LCSH: Northeastern States–Description and travel–Juvenile literature.
Classification: LCC F4.3 .W35 2024 (print) | LCC F4.3 (ebook) | DDC 917.4–dc23/eng/20230803
LC record available at https://lccn.loc.gov/2023033342
LC ebook record available at https://lccn.loc.gov/2023033343

Published in 2024 by
Enslow Publishing
2544 Clinton Street
Buffalo, NY 14224

Copyright © 2024 Enslow Publishing

Portions of this work were originally authored by Kathleen Connors and published as *Let's Explore The Northeast*. All new material in this edition is authored by Kathryn Walton.

Designer: Claire Wrazin
Editor: Natalie Humphrey

Photo credits: Series art (leather spine and corners) nevodka/Shutterstock.com, (map) Karin Hildebrand Lau/Shutterstock.com, (stamped boxes) lynea/Shutterstock.com, (old paper) Siam SK/Shutterstock.com, (vintage photo frame) shyshak roman/Shutterstock.com, (visitor's guide paper background) Andrey_Kuzmin/Shutterstock.com; cover, p. 1 (main) Mark F Lotterhand/Shutterstock.com; cover, p. 1 (inset) rck_953/Shutterstock.com; pp. 5, 21 (map) pingebat/Shutterstock.com; p. 6 StacyBirch/Shutterstock.com; p. 7 Luca Flor/Shutterstock.com; p. 9 TierneyMJ/Shutterstock.com; p. 11 (left) VDB Photos/Shutterstock.com, (right) Wangkun Jia/Shutterstock.com; p. 13 Raun Kercher/Shutterstock.com; p. 15 Jam Norasett/Shutterstock.com; p. 17 (main) on Bilous/Shutterstock.com, (inset) haveseen/Shutterstock.com; p. 19 Everett Collection/Shutterstock.com.

All rights reserved. No part of this book may be reproduced in any form without permission in writing from the publisher, except by a reviewer.

Some of the images in this book illustrate individuals who are models. The depictions do not imply actual situations or events.

Printed in the United States of America

CPSIA compliance information: Batch #CWENS24: For further information contact Enslow Publishing at 1-800-398-2504.

CONTENTS

WELCOME TO THE NORTHEAST	4
SNOW DAYS	6
NEW YORK, NEW YORK	8
MORE BIG CITIES	10
INTO THE MOUNTAINS	12
WATERWAYS	14
ADVENTURES ON THE COAST	16
FAMOUS NORTHEASTERNERS	18
SEAFOOD FOR DINNER	20
GLOSSARY	22
FOR MORE INFORMATION	23
INDEX	24

Words in the glossary appear in **bold** type the first time they are used in the text.

WELCOME TO THE NORTHEAST

The Northeast **region** of the United States is closely tied to early United States history. Many historic battles during the **American Revolution** took place there. But, if history isn't what you're looking for on a trip, the Northeast has many natural wonders and state parks to visit too.

The Northeast is made up of nine states and includes four of the largest U.S. cities. Get ready to explore this region!

• VISITOR'S GUIDE •

CONNECTICUT, MAINE, MASSACHUSETTS, NEW HAMPSHIRE, RHODE ISLAND, AND VERMONT ARE ALSO SOMETIMES CALLED NEW ENGLAND.

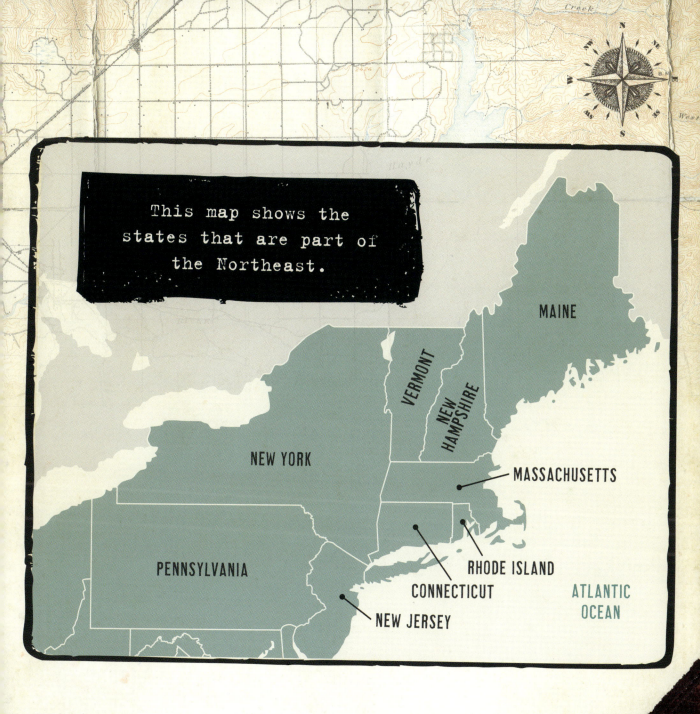

SNOW DAYS

The bodies of water close to the Northeast have a big effect on the region's weather. The nearness of the Atlantic Ocean and the Great Lakes can cause the weather to change quickly!

Bodies of water cause differences in **precipitation** too. Between 2022 and 2023, 133.6 inches (339 cm) of snow fell in Buffalo, New York, which is near two of the Great Lakes. In Albany, New York, a few hours away, it only snowed 4.7 inches (12 cm)!

• VISITOR'S GUIDE •

THE GREAT LAKES ARE FIVE **FRESHWATER** LAKES MOSTLY BETWEEN THE UNITED STATES AND CANADA. THEY ARE LAKES ERIE, HURON, MICHIGAN, ONTARIO, AND SUPERIOR.

States in the Northeast generally have four seasons.

NEW YORK, NEW YORK

New York City is the largest city in the United States. It has more **professional** sports teams in football, baseball, and basketball than any other U.S. city. While exciting events like a Yankees game or Broadway play make New York a great road-trip destination, the city is also important **internationally**. New York City is where the United Nations headquarters is located.

Visitors can also visit Ellis Island and the Statue of Liberty. There, they can learn the stories of people who came to the United States many years ago.

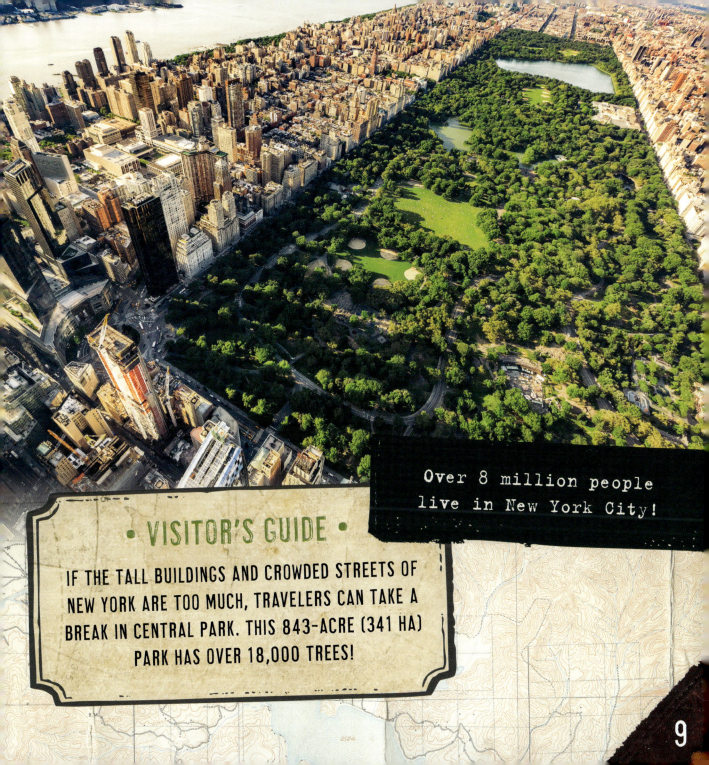

Over 8 million people live in New York City!

• VISITOR'S GUIDE •

IF THE TALL BUILDINGS AND CROWDED STREETS OF NEW YORK ARE TOO MUCH, TRAVELERS CAN TAKE A BREAK IN CENTRAL PARK. THIS 843-ACRE (341 HA) PARK HAS OVER 18,000 TREES!

MORE BIG CITIES

Philadelphia, Pennsylvania, is an important northeastern city. Independence Hall, where the U.S. **Constitution** was written, is in the heart of the city. For more history, visitors can also stop by the Liberty Bell Center to see and learn about the cracked bell.

In Boston, Massachusetts, visitors can learn about history and nature up close. They can visit the historic location of the Boston Tea Party or take a boat tour to see whales in the ocean, among other activities.

• VISITOR'S GUIDE •

THE FAMOUS STEPS FROM THE MOVIE *ROCKY* ARE IN DOWNTOWN PHILLY. THEY'RE AT THE MAIN ENTRANCE TO THE PHILADELPHIA **MUSEUM** OF ART.

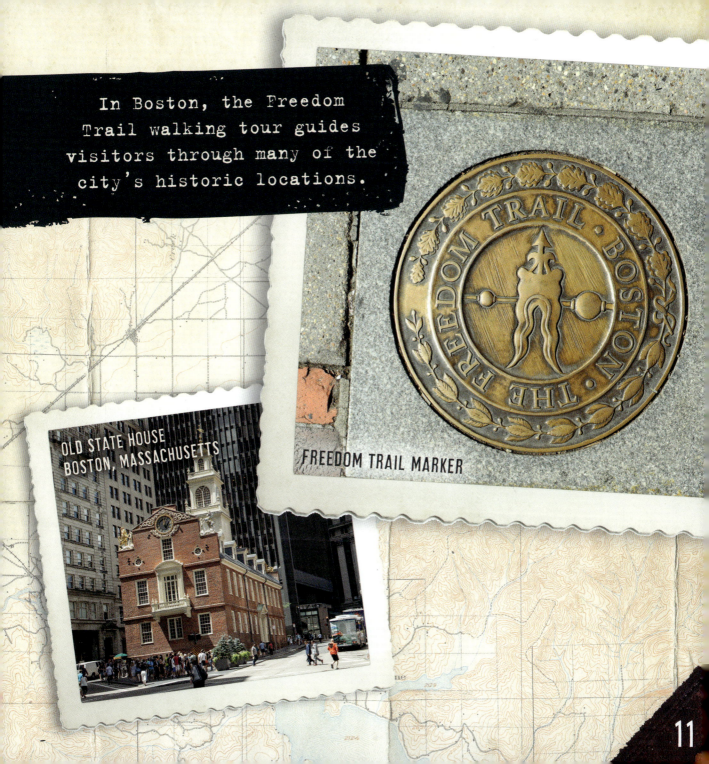

In Boston, the Freedom Trail walking tour guides visitors through many of the city's historic locations.

FREEDOM TRAIL MARKER

OLD STATE HOUSE
BOSTON, MASSACHUSETTS

INTO THE MOUNTAINS

The Northeast has many mountains to visit. The Appalachians include some of Earth's oldest mountains. Part of this range, the Green Mountains, tower over Vermont, and the White Mountains rise above New Hampshire. The Appalachians also cut through New York, Massachusetts, Connecticut, and Pennsylvania and continue south.

Many parts of the Appalachians in the Northeast are fun to visit for camping, hiking, and skiing. People hike parts of the Appalachian Trail, which begins in the Northeast and ends in Georgia.

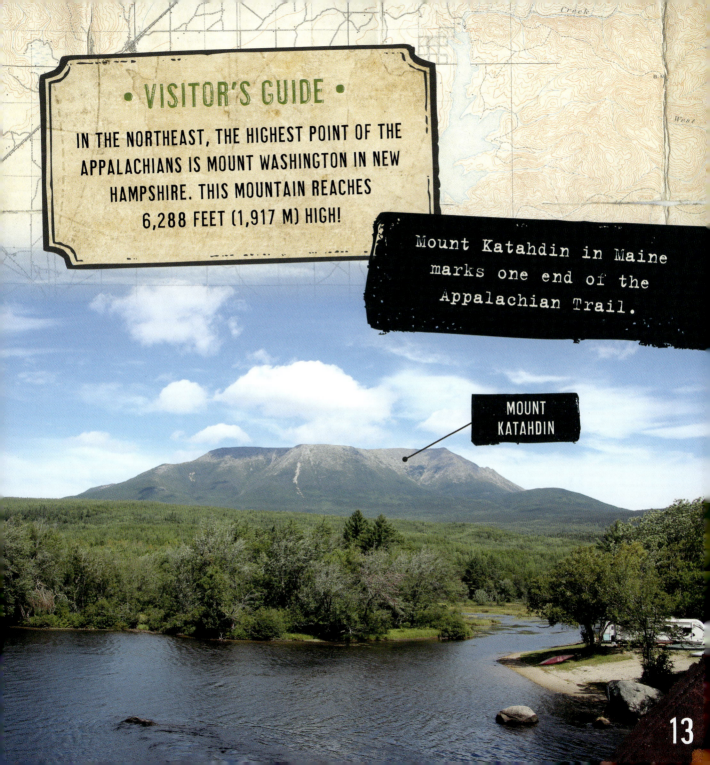

• VISITOR'S GUIDE •

IN THE NORTHEAST, THE HIGHEST POINT OF THE APPALACHIANS IS MOUNT WASHINGTON IN NEW HAMPSHIRE. THIS MOUNTAIN REACHES 6,288 FEET (1,917 M) HIGH!

Mount Katahdin in Maine marks one end of the Appalachian Trail.

MOUNT KATAHDIN

WATERWAYS

The bodies of water in the Northeast play an important role in the Northeast's history. Waterways and sites like the Hudson River and Massachusetts Bay were sources of food and **transportation**. Today, many people like to vacation on their shores!

Some waterways act as a natural border between states. Lake Champlain splits New York and Vermont, while the Delaware River divides Pennsylvania and New Jersey.

• VISITOR'S GUIDE •

NEARLY 9.5 MILLION PEOPLE VISIT NIAGARA FALLS, LOCATED BETWEEN NEW YORK STATE AND CANADA, EACH YEAR!

Over 3,000 tons (2,721.5 mt) of water flow over Niagara Falls every second.

15

ADVENTURES ON THE COAST

Except Vermont, every state in the Northeast touches the Atlantic Ocean or one of the Great Lakes. Cape Cod, Massachusetts; Bar Harbor, Maine; and Atlantic City, New Jersey, are some popular coastal spots.

In Cape Cod, visitors can climb the 252-foot (76.8 m) Pilgrim Monument. This monument is the tallest all-**granite** monument in the United States! Visitors to Acadia National Park in Maine can stop by Bar Harbor. It is a great place for nature lovers, hikers, and mountain bikers.

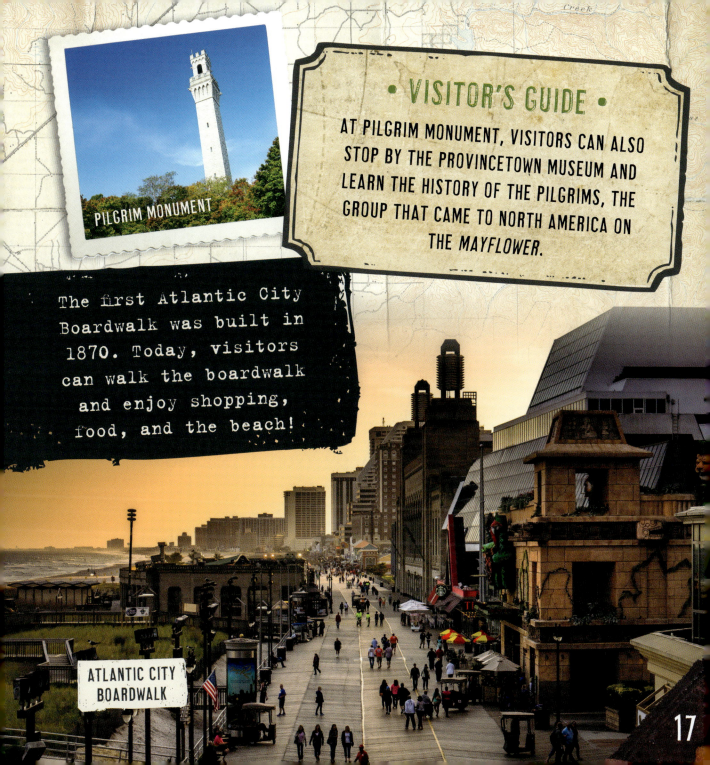

PILGRIM MONUMENT

• VISITOR'S GUIDE •

AT PILGRIM MONUMENT, VISITORS CAN ALSO STOP BY THE PROVINCETOWN MUSEUM AND LEARN THE HISTORY OF THE PILGRIMS, THE GROUP THAT CAME TO NORTH AMERICA ON THE *MAYFLOWER*.

The first Atlantic City Boardwalk was built in 1870. Today, visitors can walk the boardwalk and enjoy shopping, food, and the beach!

ATLANTIC CITY BOARDWALK

17

FAMOUS NORTHEASTERNERS

Many famous Americans were born in the Northeast. People such as presidents John F. Kennedy and George H. W. Bush were born in Massachusetts. Marvel Comics writer and editor Stan Lee was born in New York City.

Have you ever seen the painting called *Campbell's Soup Cans*? American artist Andy Warhol painted it! Warhol was born in Pittsburgh, Pennsylvania. He made his mark on modern art from the 1950s to the 1980s.

• VISITOR'S GUIDE •

THE FIGHT FOR U.S. WOMEN'S VOTING RIGHTS ALSO STARTED IN THE NORTHEAST! THE FIRST **CONVENTION** FOR WOMEN'S SUFFRAGE, OR RIGHT TO VOTE, WAS HOSTED IN 1848 IN SENECA FALLS, NEW YORK.

Susan B. Anthony, one of the first U.S. women's suffrage leaders, was born in Adams, Massachusetts.

SEAFOOD FOR DINNER

Because so many northeastern states touch the Atlantic Ocean or one of the Great Lakes, the Northeast is known for its fresh seafood. The Northeast today has some of the most **productive** fishing ports in the country! In places like New Bedford, Massachusetts, people fish millions of pounds of seafood a year.

All this fresh seafood means the Northeast serves many different seafood dishes. Visitors shouldn't miss the New England clam chowder or some crab cakes!

• VISITOR'S GUIDE •

VISITORS TO THE NORTHEAST CAN COMPARE TWO MAIN KINDS OF LOBSTER ROLLS: THE MAINE AND CONNECTICUT LOBSTER ROLLS. BOTH STATES CLAIM THEY HAVE THE BEST AROUND!

MORE THINGS TO SEE IN THE NORTHEAST

Check out more fun places to go on your trip through the Northeast!

CRAYOLA EXPERIENCE

For a colorful adventure, stop by the Crayola crayon factory in Easton, Pennsylvania.

VERMONT TEDDY BEAR FACTORY

In Shelburne, Vermont, you can see how teddy bears are made and even make your own!

SPRINGFIELD MUSEUM

At the Springfield Museum in Springfield, Massachusetts, visitors can explore art and history. They can also take a trip through the wonderful world of Dr. Seuss!

THE BIG DUCK

Visitors to Flanders, New York, can't miss this 20-foot (6 m) tall duck store.

21

GLOSSARY

American Revolution: The war in which the 13 North American colonies won their freedom from England.

constitution: The basic laws by which a country or state is governed.

convention: A gathering of people who have a common interest or purpose.

freshwater: Water that is not salty.

granite: A kind of rough, very hard rock often used for building.

international: Involving two or more countries.

museum: A building in which things of interest are displayed.

precipitation: Rain, snow, sleet, or hail.

productive: Able to make something in high amounts.

professional: Having to do with a job someone does for a living.

region: A large area of land that has features that make it different from nearby areas of land.

transportation: The act of moving people or things from one place to another.

FOR MORE INFORMATION

Books

Daly, Ruth. *Boston.* New York, NY: AV2, 2020.

Khalid, Jinnow. *The Statue of Liberty: Symbol of Freedom.* New York, NY: PowerKids Press, 2020.

Websites

Britannica Kids: The Northeast
www.kids.britannica.com/kids/article/The-Northeast/489427
Check out more interesting facts about the Northeast region.

National Geographic Kids: Native People of the American Northeast
www.kids.nationalgeographic.com/history/article/native-people-of-the-american-northeast
Learn about the people who lived in the Northeast before European settlers!

Publisher's note to educators and parents: Our editors have carefully reviewed these websites to ensure that they are suitable for students. Many websites change frequently, however, and we cannot guarantee that a site's future contents will continue to meet our high standards of quality and educational value. Be advised that students should be closely supervised whenever they access the internet.

INDEX

Acadia National Park, 16
American Revolution, 4
Appalachians, 12, 13
Atlantic Ocean, 5, 6, 16, 20
Connecticut, 4, 5, 12, 20, 21
Great Lakes, 6, 7, 16, 20
Maine, 4, 5, 13, 16, 20, 21
Massachusetts, 4, 5, 10, 11, 12, 14, 16, 18, 19, 20, 21
New Hampshire, 4, 5, 12, 13, 21
New Jersey, 5, 14, 16, 21
New York, 5, 8, 12, 14, 18, 21
Niagara Falls, 14, 15
Pennsylvania, 5, 10, 12, 14, 18, 21
Pilgrim Monument, 16, 17
Rhode Island, 4, 5, 21
Springfield Museum, 21
Statue of Liberty, 8
United Nations, 8
Vermont, 4, 5, 12, 14, 16, 21
weather, 6, 7